Examining Issues Through POLITICAL CARTOONS

World War II

Examining Issues Through
Political Cartoons

World War II

Titles in the Examining Issues Through Political Cartoons series
include:

Examining Issues Through POLITICAL CARTOONS

World War II

Edited by Laura K. Egendorf

Bruce Glassman, *Vice President*
Bonnie Szumski, *Publisher*
Helen Cothran, *Managing Editor*
Scott Barbour, *Series Editor*

GREENHAVEN PRESS
An imprint of Thomson Gale, a part of The Thomson Corporation

THOMSON
™
GALE

Detroit • New York • San Francisco • San Diego • New Haven, Conn.
Waterville, Maine • London • Munich

LIBRARY OF CONGRESS CATALOGING-IN-PUBLICATION DATA

World War II / Laura K. Egendorf, book editor.
    p. cm. — (Examining issues through political cartoons)
ISBN 0-7377-2535-4 (lib.: alk. paper)
    1. World War, 1939–1945—Caricatures and cartoons. 2. World War, 1939–1945
—Public opinion. I. Title: World War 2. II. Title: World War 2. III. Egendorf,
Laura K., 1973– . IV. Series.

D745.2.W67 2005
741.5—dc22   2004054357

Contents

Foreword

Political cartoons, also called editorial cartoons, are drawings that do what editorials do with words—express an opinion about a newsworthy event or person. They typically appear in the opinion pages of newspapers, sometimes in support of that day's written editorial, but more often making their own comment on the day's events. Political cartoons first gained widespread popularity in Great Britain and the United States in the 1800s when engravings and other drawings skewering political figures were fashionable in illustrated newspapers and comic magazines. By the beginning of the 1900s, editorial cartoons were an established feature of daily newspapers. Today, they can be found throughout the globe in newspapers, magazines, and online publications and the Internet.

Art Wood, both a cartoonist and a collector of cartoons, writes in his book *Great Cartoonists and Their Art*:

> Day in and day out the cartoonist mirrors history; he reduces complex facts into understandable and artistic terminology. He is a political commentator and at the same time an artist.

The distillation of ideas into images is what makes political cartoons a valuable resource for studying social and historical topics. Editorial cartoons have a point to express. Analyzing them involves determining both what the cartoon's point is and how it was made.

Sometimes, the point made by the cartoon may be one that the reader disagrees with, or considers offensive. Such cartoons expose readers to new ideas and thereby challenge them to analyze and question their own opinions and assumptions. In some extreme cases, cartoons provide vivid examples of the thoughts that lie behind heinous acts; for example, the cartoons created by the Nazis illustrate the anti-Semitism that led to the mass persecution of Jews.

Examining controversial ideas is but one way the study of political cartoons can enhance and develop critical thinking skills. Another aspect to cartoons is that they can use symbols to make their point quickly. For example, in a cartoon in *Euthanasia*, Chuck Asay depicts supporters of a legal "right to die" by assisted suicide as vultures. Vultures are birds that eat dead and dying animals and are often a symbol of repulsive and cowardly predators who take advantage of those who have met misfortune or are vulnerable. The reader can infer that Asay is expressing his opposition to physician-assisted suicide by suggesting that its supporters are just as loathsome as vultures. Asay thus makes his point through a quick symbolic association.

An important part of critical thinking is examining ideas and arguments in their historical context. Political cartoonists (reasonably) assume that the typical reader of a newspaper's editorial page already has a basic knowledge of current issues and newsworthy people. Understanding and appreciating political cartoons often requires such knowledge, as well as a familiarity with common icons and symbolic figures (such as Uncle Sam's representing the United States). The need for contextual information becomes especially apparent in historical cartoons. For example, although most people know who Adolf Hitler is, a lack of familiarity with other German political figures of the 1930s may create difficulty in fully understanding cartoons about Nazi Germany made in that era.

Providing such contextual information is one important way that Greenhaven's Examining Issues Through Political Cartoons series seeks to make this unique and revealing resource conveniently accessible to students. Each volume presents a representative and diverse collection of political cartoons focusing on a particular current or historical topic. An introductory essay provides a general overview of the subject matter. Each cartoon is then presented with accompanying information including facts about the cartoonist and information and commentary on the cartoon itself. Finally, each volume contains additional informational resources, including listings of books, articles, and websites; an index; and (for historical topics) a chronology of events. Taken together, the contents of each anthology constitute an amusing and informative resource for students of historical and social topics.

Introduction

The official starting date of World War II is September 1, 1939. However, the groundwork for the war had been laid from the beginning of the 1930s. Between 1931 and 1939, Germany, Italy, and Japan—the countries that would later become known as the Axis nations—behaved belligerently. For example, Germany invaded Austria in 1938, Italy conquered Ethiopia in 1936, and Japan attacked China in 1937. England's and France's initial response to these actions was appeasement, as they hoped to avoid a second world war. On September 29, 1938, English prime minister Neville Chamberlain and French premier Édouard Daladier thought they had reached an acceptable compromise with German chancellor Adolf Hitler and Italian dictator Benito Mussolini when the four men signed the Munich Agreement. The English and French heads of state agreed to give the Sudentenland (the western third of Czechoslovakia) to Germany in exchange for Germany's promise that it would not seize any more of Czechoslovakia. The Munich Agreement would soon prove to be one of the most meaningless documents in world history, as only six months later Germany ignored its pledge and conquered the rest of Czechoslovakia. Events came to a head on September 1, 1939, when Germany invaded Poland. World War II began that day and did not end until September 2, 1945, when Japan signed surrender papers. During those six years, at least 35 million people died, including 17 million troops.

In many ways World War II was similar to the wars that preceded it. It was based on arguments over land and caused misery to those on the battlefield and on the home fronts. However, World War II differed from earlier wars in several notable aspects. For example, battles occurred on three continents—Europe, Africa, and Asia—

making it a truly global war. In addition, while women had served as nurses in previous conflicts, they played a larger role in World War II, particularly in their work for the defense industry.

One of the most significant factors that made World War II truly unique, though, was the use of increasingly advanced technology. Sometimes this technology was merely an improvement of earlier equipment, such as more efficient tanks and fighter planes. In other cases new inventions emerged, notably radar, computers, and the atomic bomb. The end result was that war was no longer fought just in the trenches—though battles on the ground remained a part of war—but was also fought in the air and behind the front lines. Subsequent wars have followed the same path, though with ever-advancing technology.

Building Better Tanks

The equipment used by soldiers has steadily improved throughout history, from spears to bows and arrows to rifles to automatic weapons. One piece of equipment that was greatly improved during World War II was the tank.

When first used during World War I, the average tank could travel ten miles per hour. By World War II the typical German tank, or panzer, could travel four times as fast. Guns were mounted onto turrets that rotated 360 degrees, thus enabling soldiers in the tank to fire in any direction. Throughout the war Germany built tanks that were equipped with thicker armor and more powerful guns, which made them mightier but at the same time slower and more vulnerable to attack. Despite those drawbacks, German tanks were far superior to those used by the Allies during the first few years of the war.

Russia, Great Britain, and the United States gradually replaced their less powerful tanks as the war continued. The Russian military designed two new tanks, the KV-1 and the T-34/76; both tanks had armament superior to that of the panzers and had armored hulls that could withstand almost all German guns. Great Britain, who had initially used tanks whose weapons were too weak to pierce the panzers and whose own thin armor made them vulnerable to attack, added more powerful guns and thicker armor to tanks sent from the United States. American troops relied largely on Sherman tanks, fast machines that, like all tanks, could not withstand attacks from the air but had the advantage of being well built and easy to repair, unlike Germany's tanks.

Tanks took on a new purpose in World War II and in the conflicts that have followed. The opposing armies in World War I had dug trenches; the fighting took place in the area between the trenches known as "no man's land." Tanks were utilized primarily to end the stalemates created by this type of warfare. Crossing no man's land was dangerous for foot soldiers, but it was a trip that a tank could make easily. Tanks traveled between the trenches and withstood enemy mortar, which allowed the soldiers it transported to continue fighting and thus broke the stalemates. Trench warfare was largely eliminated in World War II; the faster and more powerful tanks used during that war operated independent of the infantry. Today tanks are even more technologically advanced, with equipment that includes powerful cannons, night-vision devices, and computerized controls.

Battles at Sea: Submarines

The development of submarines during the twentieth century parallels that of tanks. Germany had used submarines (U-boats) during World War I, primarily to sink British merchant ships that transported war materials. As with tanks, the German submarines utilized during World War II were superior to any weapon the Allies could counter with. During the war the Germans relied on two types of submarines: U-boats, which weighed two hundred tons and traveled at the speed of twenty knots when they were at the surface and six knots when submerged; and larger submarines that weighed twenty-one hundred tons and were equipped with up to nineteen torpedoes. The U-boats sank more than forty-seven hundred Allied boats, a catastrophe during the early years of the war. Harvard University professor and navy rear admiral Samuel Eliot Morison wrote in *The Two-Ocean War*: "The massacre enjoyed by the U-boats along our Atlantic Coast in 1942 was as much a national disaster as if saboteurs had destroyed half a dozen of our biggest war plants."[1]

By comparison, the typical American submarines weighed 1,450 tons and were equipped with one gun, several automatic weapons, and ten torpedoes. They could travel at seventeen knots at the surface and half that fast beneath the surface. Their slower speed and smaller amount of weaponry made these submarines vulnerable to attack both from planes and from German submarines.

What ultimately led to American superiority in the water was the addition of sonar and radar to submarines. Sonar was used to locate submerged submarines, while radar helped the Allies detect submarines that had surfaced. The development of sonar began after World War I, but it was not a reliable tool until World War II. Sonar works via high-frequency sound waves, which find objects underwater through echo tracking. Radar also relies on waves, in this case radio waves. Developed by the British in 1939, radar locates moving objects by bouncing radio waves off them. Waves then bounce back to the radar, which has receivers that can indicate the locations and distances of the objects.

The creation of sonar and radar was a huge asset to the Allies. Ships used sonar to locate and destroy submerged German submarines, while airplanes used radar to find subs nearer to the surface. This development ended Germany's early domination in naval battles. Radar also assisted the Allies in the Pacific theater by enabling American ships to detect Japanese airplanes. Intriguingly, radars can detect other radars, which can then be stolen or destroyed, thereby further weakening the opposition.

Advances in Fighter Planes

The equipment that improved the most technologically during World War II was the airplane. Planes were a nascent technology during World War I, having been invented only a dozen years earlier. During that war, fighter pilots flew wooden biplanes equipped with forward-firing machine guns. The wooden biplanes of World War I were replaced by steel monoplanes that could fly farther and faster than their predecessors.

Airplanes were an essential element of the German war strategy known as blitzkrieg, or "lightning war." The idea behind this strategy was to overwhelm the enemy by striking it with air and ground forces simultaneously. The German air force, or *Luftwaffe*, was exceptional at this task. Most German pilots flew the Me-109, which could reach speeds of 354 miles per hour.

Germany also led the way in the development of jets. Planes had previously been powered by propellers. With jet propulsion, the gases that are exhausted during the burning of fuel propel the aircraft. In 1942 the Messerschmitt factory built the first plane that used jet propulsion, the Me-262A. These planes were faster than any flown by Allied pilots and thus especially well suited for fighting. However, German efforts to further develop jet propulsion were stymied by Hitler. Germany's leader requested that the jet airplanes be converted into bombers. Unfortunately for the Germans these revamped planes were slower, and thus easier to destroy. Jet engines were also used in self-guided rockets which dropped one-ton explosives.

Germany's air superiority was tested before the development of the jet in 1942, however, during one of the turning points of the war: the Battle of Britain. For two months, from July to September 1940 (with bombing of London continuing until May 1941), the *Luftwaffe* blitzed England in hopes that the attacks would dishearten the British populace and spur them into asking their government to surrender. However, while homes, businesses, and historical landmarks were destroyed, Britain was not intimidated. This battle proved to be the first major triumph of the Allies, showing the courage and tenacity of Britain's pilots as well as the British citizens.

Royal Air Force pilots flew Hawker Hurricanes and Supermarine Spitfires, both of which were as powerful as Germany's Me-109s. The Spitfire could fly as fast as 360 miles per hour and reach an altitude of thirty-four thousand feet. That plane was used against the German fighters, while the slower Hurricanes faced off against German bombers. By striking down German planes, the RAF was able to weaken the *Luftwaffe* and thus reduce the amount of damage of the Blitzkrieg.

Richard Hough and Denis Richards, in their book *The Battle of Britain*, explain that the RAF succeeded because its pilots were well trained, skillful, and led ably by Commander in Chief Sir Hugh Dowding. While they note that the civilian population of Britain was a tremendous resource during the battle, assisting in rebuilding damaged aircraft and working the radar stations, the authors conclude, "When tribute is duly paid to the many contributors to the victory who are sometimes overlooked or forgotten, the mind rightly and inevitably comes back to those superb fighter pilots and their commander-in-chief."[2]

In the Pacific theater, Japanese pilots flew the Mitsubishi A6M Type O fighter plane, nicknamed "Zero" by the Allies. It was equipped with two guns and a cannon, could fly 330 miles per hour, and could travel nineteen hundred miles without refueling. The United States initially countered with the Grumman F4F Wildcat, which was slower than the Zero and could go only 770 miles before refueling.

However, the quality of American warplanes improved greatly during World War II. In the Pacific, the F4F Wildcat was replaced by the F6F-5 Hellcat, which was more powerful than the Zero. The two planes used most in Europe were the Republic P-47 Thunderbolt and the North American P-51 Mustang. If equipped with a spare fuel tank, the latter plane could fly round-trip from England to Germany. British and American ingenuity combined to make the Mustang even more powerful—engines produced by British car manufacturer Rolls Royce enabled the plane to reach 440 miles per hour.

The development of planes during World War II permanently changed the way wars have been fought. Recognizing the value of aircraft, the United States established the U.S. Air Force in 1947—prior to that, the air force had been controlled by the army. Air strikes have been a major element of wars from Korea to Iraq. However, while planes are faster and more powerful than before, they can never completely supplant ground combat.

Code-Breaking Computers

Tanks, submarines, and planes are examples of tools of war that benefited from improved technology. However, an entirely new technology—computers—emerged during World War II. Computers proved invaluable due to their role in code breaking. By deciphering the codes of the Axis armies, the Allied troops were better able to strategize and prepare for battle.

Colossus was the name given to one of those wartime computers. While primitive in comparison to today's machines, Colossus still allowed for faster computations than humans alone could muster, and because it was a "parallel" computer it could work on several problems at the same time. The computer, which was located in Bletchley Park in Britain, helped break Germany's Lorenz Cipher. Also known as "Fish," the cipher had been used by the Nazi high command to encode messages. According to reporter David Jamieson, Colossus was an invaluable asset. He writes, "Cracking the Fish cipher gave the allies access to the highest grade signals intelligence ever produced during wartime. Without it, the D-day landings would have been a disaster. It's estimated the invention of this first computer reduced the length of World War II by three years."[3]

Another computer used during wartime was the Mark I, the first large-scale general purpose digital computer produced in the United States. The computer was built between 1939 and 1944 and was leased upon completion by the U.S. Navy, which used it for ballistics and gunnery calculations.

Modern wars would be nearly impossible to fight without computers. Their uses include launching missiles and transmitting information via e-mail. In addition computerized consoles help soldiers navigate their tanks and Humvees, while satellite positioning technology makes it easier for commanders to determine where to send troops.

The Dawn of the Atomic Age

While the above technologies greatly influenced the progress of World War II, no advancement had quite as great an impact as did the creation of the atomic bomb. Although the first bombs were not dropped until August 1945, research into the possibility began long before the United States entered World War II. In the early 1930s physicists made several important discoveries that made the atomic bomb possible. In 1932 J.D. Cockroft and E.T.S. Walton became the first people to split an atom, turning a lithium nucleus into two helium nuclei by bombarding the nucleus with protons. Two years later the Italian physicist Enrico Fermi used neutrons instead of protons and discovered that slow-moving neutrons were more effective at creating radioactive atoms. In 1938 these slow neutrons led to the discovery of nuclear fission by Otto Hahn and Fritz Strassman. The scientists used the neutrons to split an isotope of uranium.

President Franklin D. Roosevelt became involved in atomic advancements six weeks after World War II began. Although the United States was still neutral at the time, the president formed a committee to study uranium, believing that the United States could not allow Hitler to create a weapon more powerful than any the Allies had in their arsenal. On January 19, 1942, Roosevelt approved the development of the atomic bomb. This decision followed several advances by scientists, among them the discovery of fissionable plutonium.

The atomic bomb was developed over the next three and a half years by the Manhattan Project, whose principal members included Fermi and Robert Oppenheimer. In early December 1942, the first self-sustained nuclear chain reaction took place in a laboratory in the basement of the University of Chicago football field. By 1944 models of atomic bombs were being tested in Los Alamos, New Mexico. That town was also the site of a successful test of a plutonium bomb on July 16, 1945.

President Harry Truman, who took office after Roosevelt died, heard the results of the test eight days later, while at the Potsdam Conference. He authorized the use of the atomic bomb on Japan because it appeared that Japan would not surrender unconditionally otherwise. The president also felt that dropping the bombs would spare the hundreds of thousands of American and Japanese lives that would be lost if the war continued. Thus, on August 6, 1945, a uranium bomb was released above Hiroshima, and three days later an American pilot dropped a plutonium bomb on Nagasaki.

Six decades later Truman's decision remains arguably the most controversial ever made by a world leader during a war. The devastation caused by the bombs, both their immediate impact on the two cities and the lingering effects of radiation, alerted the world to the dangers of this new technology. Although several countries possess nuclear weapons, the leaders of these nations, recognizing the devastating potential of the atom, have refrained from using them. The danger is still present, however, and the existence of atomic energy leaves many people fearful that Hiroshima and Nagasaki will not be the only two cities destroyed by nuclear weapons.

Beyond World War II

World War II changed the way wars were fought. Tanks and submarines moved faster than in earlier wars, while airplanes became an integral part of combat. In World War II and the wars that followed, battles on the ground remained crucial—there is still no better way to take control of a city or nation—but there was now a heightened reliance on bombing the enemy into submission. At the same time, the existence of atomic bombs has led to efforts to prevent another worldwide war. Technology continues to be an increasingly crucial element of warfare, with the development of more sophisticated computers and communication tools.

World War II was the most important event of the twentieth century, not only because of the technology that developed but because of the way it changed the world politically, economically, and socially. In the following chapters of *Examining Issues Through Political Cartoons: World War II*, cartoonists examine various aspects of the war: "Heroes and Villains," "Perspectives on the War," "The Home Front," and "Aftermath." The selections in this volume help provide insight into the people and events that made World War II the epochal era that it was.

Notes

1. Samuel Eliot Morison, *The Two-Ocean War*. Boston: Little, Brown, 1963.

2. Richard Hough and Denis Richards, *The Battle of Britain*. New York: W.W. Norton, 1989.

3. David Jamieson, "Computers and Espionage," April 12, 2001. www.bbcworld.com/content/clickonline_archive_15_2001.asp? pageid=666&co_pageid=3.

Chapter 1

Heroes
and Villains

EXAMINING ISSUES THROUGH
POLITICAL CARTOONS

Preface

In February 1945 Franklin Roosevelt, Winston Churchill, and Joseph Stalin met at Yalta to discuss how Germany would be divided once the Allies had won World War II. Five months later, the leaders of the United States, Great Britain, and the Soviet Union again gathered, this time in Potsdam, to make more plans for the postwar era. However, Roosevelt had died in April and had been succeeded by Harry Truman. Churchill began the Potsdam Conference as Britain's prime minister but was forced to leave partway through, as he lost an election to Labour Party leader Clement Atlee, who took his place in Potsdam. This turn of events is particularly surprising because Winston Churchill's oratorical skills and his ability to rouse the spirits of the British during the darkest days of the war made him one of the heroes of World War II.

Churchill had a long career in British politics, receiving his first cabinet post in 1908. On May 10, 1940, following Prime Minister Neville Chamberlain's resignation (the same day that Germany invaded Holland and Belgium), King George VI asked Churchill to replace Chamberlain. Churchill thus came to power at one of the most difficult times in British history. Western Europe was rapidly falling to Germany, and the United States was remaining neutral. Though Britain had other allies, including Australia and Canada, it was up to the small island nation to prevent Germany from reaching the Atlantic Ocean.

During the summer of 1940, Churchill rallied the spirits of his nation in a series of legendary speeches. His writing skills were unquestioned—in fact, Churchill won a Nobel Prize for Literature in 1953—but so too was his ability to deliver those words forcefully. His words were especially necessary because May through September

1940 were difficult months. In addition to the fall of other European nations, including France on June 22, Britain had to withstand more than two months of bombing attacks in the Battle of Britain. From July 10 through September 15, 1940, the German air force (Luftwaffe) dropped thousands of bombs on English cities. London was blitzed until May 1941. Despite the onslaught, Britain won the battle and staved off a Nazi invasion.

An example of Churchill's oratory is the speech he delivered on August 20, 1940, before the House of Commons. The prime minister discusses the struggles of the coming years, at the same time appealing to the honor of his nation, declaring, "When we are doing the finest thing in the world, and have the honor to be the sole champion of the liberties of all Europe, we must not grudge these years or weary as we toil and struggle through them." Churchill goes on to laud the bravery of the Royal Air Force and its efforts in the Battle of Britain. Some of Churchill's most famous words are in praise of the British airmen. He asserts: "[The airmen] are turning the tide of the World War by their prowess and by their devotion. Never in the field of human conflict was so much owed by so many to so few." This speech is an example of the way Churchill lauded all elements of Britain's war effort.

However, Churchill's importance during World War II went well beyond his ability to deliver speeches. As Britain's commander in chief, he oversaw every aspect of the war effort. His key achievements included developing a strong relationship with Franklin Roosevelt, resulting in the Lend-Lease Act, under which the United States agreed to send supplies to Britain and any other nation fighting Germany.

The irony for Churchill is that while he was able to rally Britain behind the war, he was not so skilled at gathering public support for his domestic policies. Distaste for Churchill's views on health care and education, as well as the social policies of the Conservatives as a whole, helped lead to his defeat. Churchill won more votes than Atlee, but the Labour Party garnered an overall majority, and thus Churchill was supplanted. However, Churchill would eventually regain power and return to 10 Downing Street from 1951 to 1955.

Like the other heroes and villains of World War II, Winston Churchill was a complicated and charismatic person. In this chapter the cartoonists offer their views on some of the crucial figures of the war, including Churchill, Roosevelt, and Adolf Hitler.

Examining Cartoon 1:

"Rendezvous"

Hitler   **RENDEZVOUS**   Stalin

About the Cartoon

On August 23, 1939, Germany and the Soviet Union signed the Molotov-Ribbentrop Pact. Although the treaty was ostensibly a nonaggression agreement, the two nations secretly agreed to divide eastern Europe. Their desires became clear the following month, when Germany instigated World War II by invading Poland on September 1 and the Soviet Union launched its own attack on the eastern European nation on September 17. The pact eventually ended, when Germany invaded the Soviet Union in June 1941 and the Soviet Union joined the Allied forces.

The men who led Germany and the Soviet Union during World War II were Adolf Hitler and Joseph Stalin, respectively. Both men are among the most infamous leaders of the twentieth century. In

23

this cartoon David Low shows Hitler and Stalin standing over the body of a Polish man, which represents their mutual destruction of Poland. The two leaders gesture politely—bowing and removing their hats—but their words reveal they have little respect for each other. Hitler views Stalin as "scum of the earth," while Stalin believes that Hitler is an "assassin of the workers." Low appears to be suggesting that the pact between Germany and the Soviet Union is a marriage of political convenience and that the two leaders and their two nations will not be able to fully ally.

About the Cartoonist

David Low was a political cartoonist for the London newspaper *Evening Standard* during the 1930s and 1940s.

Examining Cartoon 2:
"The Dragonslayer"

About the Cartoon

Winston Churchill, who served as Great Britain's prime minister through most of World War II, is one of the most memorable leaders in world history. His early stance against appeasing Adolf Hitler in the 1930s set him apart from then–prime minister Neville Chamberlain, while Churchill's impassioned oratory during the war rallied both the British civilians and military. In this cartoon E.H. Shepard depicts the prime minister as a modern-day version of England's patron saint, Saint George. George was a knight who was legendary for killing dragons; hence, the imagery of Churchill decked in armor, standing in triumph over a slain beast (representing Germany). The cartoonist is suggesting that the prime minister is England's new protector. This cartoon was published on January 1, 1941, when the United States had yet to enter the war and Germany had conquered most of western Europe, with Great Britain being the major exception.

About the Cartoonist

E.H. Shepard was a cartoonist for the British humor magazine *Punch* from 1907 to 1958.

Examining Cartoon 3:
"Franklin Roosevelt"

About the Cartoon

President Franklin Delano Roosevelt led the United States during twelve of the most difficult years in American history, from the Great Depression through World War II. Early in his fourth term, several weeks before Germany surrendered and the war in Europe concluded, Roosevelt died of a cerebral hemorrhage. Jerry Doyle honors the memory of the president in this cartoon. By referring to the president as having "died in action," Doyle is equating Roosevelt with the soldiers who have lost their lives since the war began. He also shows the extent to which Roosevelt was respected throughout the world via the imagery of the flags of the Allied nations at half-mast.

About the Cartoonist

Jerry Doyle was a cartoonist for the *Philadelphia Record* who was known for depicting Roosevelt as a larger-than-life figure.

Chapter 2

Perspectives on the War

Preface

Censorship is a four-letter word to journalists. During wars, however, radio, television, and print reporters recognize that their nation's soldiers might be placed in danger if details of war plans are published or broadcast. Censorship of the media, both voluntary and mandatory, was a common occurrence during World War II on both sides of the Atlantic.

The U.S. government took steps to control communication during the war. The First War Powers Act, passed ten days after the United States entered World War II, granted President Franklin D. Roosevelt the authority to censor "communications by mail, cable, radio, or other means of transmission passing between the United States and any foreign country." The president also established an Office of Censorship, whose employees examined thousands of public and private communications and established guidelines for voluntary news censorship, the Code of Wartime Practices for the American Press. In his introduction to his book *Secrets of Victory*, Michael S. Sweeney writes, "journalists . . . were willing to cooperate and do their part [for the war]. The public did not see journalists (and journalists did not see themselves) as being against the team. Journalists were part of the team."

While American journalists did not intentionally violate the rules of reporting established during World War II, these proscriptions could not ensure that journalists never wrote articles that might endanger American troops. Sweeney explains, "Journalists who had not received a copy of the censorship code, or had not read it, or had not understood it, violated it in many ways, from revealing the departure of troop units to giving the location and nature of stateside war industries. What did not occur was a wholesale sabotage of censorship for personal or corporate gain."

The American government was not alone in censoring wartime journalists. Similar acts occurred in other Allied nations, such as England and Canada. None of these nations, however, went as far as Nazi Germany. Free press was illegal in the nations conquered by the Axis troops—newspapers and radio stations were either closed down or placed under Nazi control. Propaganda replaced the independent press, with articles and cartoons supporting the goals of Adolf Hitler and excoriating the acts of the Allies and the Jews. People in occupied lands that were found publishing, listening to, or reading unauthorized materials could face severe penalties, including death.

Censorship can make finding unfettered reporting on wars difficult. However, columnists and cartoonists are frequently able to express perspectives that may not be acceptable in other formats. In this chapter cartoonists from several of the nations involved in World War II provide their unique points of view on the events and morality of the war.

Examining Cartoon 1:
"John Bull's War Aim"

About the Cartoon

One of the most memorable moments in cinema is that of King Kong grabbing Ann Darrow and climbing up the Empire State Building. Bernard Partridge uses that image in this cartoon to show England's courage in the early stages of the war. The notation that Partridge is following the style of French sculptor Emmanuel Frémiet likely refers to Frémiet's use of animal figures in his sculptures.

With the United States remaining largely neutral for the first two years of World War II, it fell on Great Britain to protect western Europe from Germany. In this cartoon "John Bull"—the British equivalent of Uncle Sam—aims a gun at Partridge's version of King Kong, one who has facial features resembling German chancellor Adolf Hitler and wears a Nazi swastika armband. The helpless damsel symbolizes freedom, which must be rescued by the British military and government.

About the Cartoonist

Bernard Partridge was the chief cartoonist for the British humor magazine *Punch* from 1901 until his death in 1945.

Examining Cartoon 2:
"Atlantic Sea Serpent"

Atlantic Sea Serpent

About the Cartoon

The United States declared war on Japan on December 8, 1941, one day after the Japanese air attack on the naval installation in Pearl Harbor, Hawaii. With Adolf Hitler declaring war on the United States soon after, Americans found themselves at war in both Europe and the Pacific. In this cartoon Eugene Elderman shows how the U.S. military had to make sure that it did not focus so intently on one theater of war that it neglected the dangers posed by the other. While the United States, represented by the figure of Uncle Sam, tries to focus on the battles in the Pacific, it is also aware of the dangers from the Atlantic, which are represented by a dragon named "Nazi Subs." German submarines, also known as U-boats, were largely responsible for the sinking of more than forty-seven hundred Allied and neutral nations' boats.

About the Cartoonist

Eugene Elderman was a cartoonist for the *Washington Post*.

Examining Cartoon 3:
"Who Is Who"

About the Cartoon

Nazi Germany was perhaps best known for its anti-Semitism; the Nazi government and most of its citizens blamed the Jews for Germany's social and economic problems in the decades following the nation's defeat in the first World War. This hatred would eventually lead to the Holocaust and the death of 6 million European Jews. In their World War II propaganda, German writers and cartoonists frequently alleged that Jews were controlling the war efforts of the Allies. In this cartoon, the cartoonist Waldl shows who he thinks is behind the attacks on Germany. The first panel depicts British prime minister Winston Churchill as the puppet master. The second panel reveals that Churchill himself is a puppet on the arm of U.S. president Franklin Delano Roosevelt. Finally, the third panel shows a man with stereotypically Semitic features, such as dark, bushy hair and a hooked nose. No name is given for the obviously Jewish man, but the four blank letters likely stand for Jude, which is German for Jewish.

About the Cartoonist

Waldl was the pseudonym of Walter Hofmann, an illustrator for *Das Schwarze Korps*, a journal published by the Schutzstaffel (Protective Squad), or SS, which was Adolf Hitler's private army.

Waldl. © 1941 by *Folge*. Reproduced by permission.

Examining Cartoon 4:
"American Imperialism"

About the Cartoon

Japan began to flex its power in Asia in the 1930s. In 1931 the nation invaded Manchuria, followed in 1937 by an attack on China and two years later by the seizure of Hainan Island. In December 1941 Japan invaded the Philippines, which had previously been a U.S. colony but was moving toward independence. This anonymous drawing from a Japanese propaganda leaflet that was intended for English-speaking Filipinos argues that Japan is rescuing Filipinos (represented by a figure named Juan) from the circling sharks of American imperialism and racial prejudice. In truth the Japanese occupation was particularly violent and cruel. The U.S. military drove Japan out of the Philippines during the final months of World War II.

Japanese leaflet to English-speaking Filipinos, 1941.

Examining Cartoon 5:
"Very Much Alive!"

About the Cartoon

France surrendered to Germany on June 22, 1940. However, an underground resistance movement soon developed in the nation. Led by Communists, Socialists, and soldiers who had escaped Nazi imprisonment, the movement—which consisted of several groups —worked secretly to aid the Allies. The French resistance was united under General Charles de Gaulle in 1943. The resistance played a significant role during the D-day invasion and proved invaluable to the Allies' victory in Europe.

In this cartoon, published thirteen months after France's surrender, Philip Zec depicts Adolf Hitler sitting on top of a coffin that represents France. Hitler is startled when he sees an arm reach out of the coffin and write a "V" on the wall. The V stands for victory, indicating that France still has life in it.

About the Cartoonist

Philip Zec was a cartoonist for the *Daily Mirror*, a London newspaper. He was known for his powerful and frequently controversial drawings.

Examining Cartoon 6:
"Fresh, Spirited American Troops"

Fresh, spirited American troops, flushed with victory, are bringing in thousands of hungry, ragged, battle-weary prisoners.

About the Cartoon

World War II was difficult for both the victors and the losers, as this cartoon by Bill Mauldin suggests. The caption for the cartoon mentions "spirited American troops" and "battle-weary prisoners." In this drawing, however, it is nearly impossible to tell the two groups apart. All the men appear exhausted, with no signs of victory on the face of the American soldier. One German soldier, with his right arm in a sling, appears to be looking at his captor with empathy. Mauldin's drawing indicates that all of the people fighting in World War II are suffering equally.

About the Cartoonist

Bill Mauldin was one of the most famous World War II cartoonists. His cartoons focused on adventures and frustrations of the cynical soldiers "Willie" and "Joe" and were published by the military newspaper *Stars and Stripes*. Mauldin also worked as a political cartoonist for the *St. Louis Post-Dispatch* and the *Chicago Sun-Times* and won Pulitzer Prizes in 1945 and 1959. Anthologies of Mauldin's cartoons include *Up Front* and *A Sort of Saga*.

Chapter 3

The Home Front

EXAMINING ISSUES THROUGH
POLITICAL CARTOONS

Preface

F amilies on the home front during World War II made numerous changes to their lives in order to support the war effort. They purchased bonds, participated in scrap metal drives, and accepted the censorship of letters sent between America and the battlefields. One aspect of life in the United States that was significantly altered by World War II was the American diet. Food rationing altered the way Americans ate, both during and after the war.

Americans faced significant restrictions in the foods they purchased because the U.S. government had to be certain that it could provide sufficient food for the millions of soldiers serving overseas. Coffee and sugar were among the first items to be rationed. In 1943 canned goods, meat, fish, and dairy were added to the list. Americans on the home front used coupons issued by the Office of Price Administration to buy these and other rationed goods.

Rationing compelled Americans to change their diet in several ways. They relied more heavily on foods that could be purchased without coupons, such as produce and cereals. Vegetables were also grown in the "victory gardens" that were planted in backyards and at schools. Readily available and inexpensive foods began to be substituted for those that could only be acquired in small amounts. For example, margarine became a substitute for butter, while many Americans turned to cottage cheese, boxed macaroni and cheese, organ meats, and the canned meat product Spam as replacements for steaks and other expensive cuts of beef. Not everyone gave up their prewar diet so readily, though—a black market emerged during the war, offering meat and other coveted foods for those able and willing to afford them.

British civilians participated in rationing as well, further showing the willingness of those on the home front to support the efforts of their soldiers. Civilians during World War II were perhaps more united than in any war before or since. In the following chapter the cartoonists examine the attitudes of the men and women on the American and British home fronts.

Examining Cartoon 1:
"Spreading the Lovely Goebbels Stuff"

About the Cartoon

Charles A. Lindbergh achieved international fame in 1927 when he successfully completed a solo flight across the Atlantic Ocean. However, in the 1930s he also became known for being an isolationist, or someone who did not believe the United States should become involved in foreign wars. Lindbergh shared these views with his fellow members in the America First Committee (AFC), an organization that believed the United States should stay out of European conflicts because it feared that intervention could lead to the spread of socialism, communism, and fascism. Lindbergh went so far as to suggest in January 1941 that the United States negotiate a neutrality pact with Adolf Hitler. The fondness between Lindbergh and Nazi Germany was mutual—in 1938 Lindbergh accepted a medal of honor from Hermann Göring, one of Hitler's top aides.

Like those of many members of the AFC, Lindbergh's views were coupled with anti-Semitism and pro-Nazism, a fact that Theodor Geisel decries in this cartoon. Lindbergh is depicted standing on top of a dump truck shoveling trash while wearing a mask in order to avoid the stench. The truck is driven by a Nazi, as indicated by the swastika on his arm, and is labeled "Nazi Anti-Semite Stink Wagon." The label makes Geisel's views on the propaganda spread by Lindbergh and other Nazi sympathizers clear. The title of the cartoon refers to Nazi propaganda minister Joseph Goebbels, who helped spread those repugnant beliefs. This cartoon was published prior to the attack on Pearl Harbor, after which Lindbergh supported America's entry into World War II.

About the Cartoonist

Theodor Geisel, or Dr. Seuss, is best known for his beloved children's books. During World War II he drew political cartoons for *PM* magazine.

Examining Cartoon 2:
"United States"

UNITED STATES

About the Cartoon

On December 7, 1941, Japanese warplanes launched an attack on
Pearl Harbor, the U.S. naval installation that was based at Oahu,
Hawaii. The attack destroyed or damaged twenty-one vessels,
killed 2,388 people, and wounded another two thousand troops.
The incident prompted the United States to enter World War II;
before that, America's involvement in the war had been limited to
providing military aid to Great Britain. This cartoon by Victor
Weisz, published three days after the attack, shows how Americans
from varied political backgrounds supported the U.S. government's
decision. The bombing at Pearl Harbor had, as the title's play on
words suggests, literally "united" the nation.

The man standing at the front of the group is President Franklin D. Roosevelt. The man standing at his right is Fiorello La Guardia, the Republican mayor of New York City who often disagreed with Roosevelt politically but stood behind the president during the war. As the mayor of the nation's largest city and the president of the U.S. Conference of Mayors, La Guardia was an important figure. To the other side of Roosevelt is John L. Lewis, the president of the United Mine Workers of America and the founding president of the Congress of Industrial Organizations. Former president Herbert Hoover is positioned behind Lewis. During the war Hoover established relief committees that provided food to struggling European democracies. Despite losing to Roosevelt in the 1940 presidential election, Wendell Willkie, who is standing behind La Guardia, was a strong supporter of FDR's foreign policies and toured England, China, the Soviet Union, and the Middle East during 1941 and 1942 as the president's personal representative. Next to Willkie is newspaper magnate William Randolph Hearst. Although Hearst was critical of Roosevelt's domestic fiscal policies, he also put aside those views in support of the president and the war. The final figure in the cartoon is aviator Charles Lindbergh. Lindbergh was a staunch isolationist until Pearl Harbor. With this unified show of support, the United States was ready to battle Japan and Germany, which are represented by the two figures in the bottom corner—German chancellor Adolf Hitler and Japanese prime minister Hideki Tojo.

About the Cartoonist

Victor Weisz, who signed his cartoons "Vicky," was a German Jew who left his homeland following Adolf Hitler's rise to power. He arrived in England in 1935 and worked as a political cartoonist for several publications, including the London-based *News Chronicle*. Anthologies of his work include *Aftermath: Cartoons by Vicky* and *Vicky's World*.

Examining Cartoon 3:
"Letting the Genie Out of the Bottle"

About the Cartoon

One of the major effects of World War II on the home front was the way it changed the demographics of the U.S. workforce. In particular the departure of the 16 million men who served in the American military during World War II opened up new economic opportunities for American women. During the war, the number of working women rocketed from 12 million to 19 million. Many of these women chose to help with the war effort by taking jobs in the defense industry, such as in shipyards and aircraft factories; they were symbolized by the wartime character "Rosie the Riveter."

While the women who worked in the factories were respected for their contribution to the war effort, attitudes began to shift once it became clear that the United States and its allies would defeat the German-Japan-Italian axis. Women were urged to leave the workforce and return to domestic life as soon as their husbands and boyfriends came home. Many women did go back to their traditional roles, as the rise in births in the years after the war (the "baby boom") attests. Still, as this cartoon by J.N. "Ding" Darling suggests, it was nearly impossible to put the genie back into the bottle—that is, to convince all of the working women to give up their increased salaries and return to their previous status. Working on behalf of the war made American women feel more important, as indicated by the figure of the giant woman. In a gender switch, she wears overalls and holds a lunch pail and tools while looking down derisively at the apron-wearing man who holds a broom and frying pan.

About the Cartoonist

J.N. "Ding" Darling was one of the most respected political cartoonists of the twentieth century, with his work syndicated in 150 newspapers. His career spanned from 1912 to 1962 and included two Pulitzer Prizes.

Examining Cartoon 4:
"No Privacy!"

"No privacy! No privacy!"

About the Cartoon

For months in 1940 and 1941, England—in particular London—withstood intensive bombings by German fighter planes. Germany had hoped that the bombs would intimidate English civilians and reduce support for Britain's fight against Germany, but their tactic failed. Despite the fatalities, extensive disruptions, and damage created by the bombs, Britons famously went on with their lives, displaying their "stiff upper lips." They were largely inspired to do so by their king and queen, who steadfastly remained in London instead of seeking refuge in Scotland.

David Langdon salutes the ability of the English to continue on with their lives in the accompanying cartoon. Despite having the front of their house ripped away by a bomb, a husband and wife eat breakfast and bemoan their lack of privacy. The man is upset by the presence of inspectors, who have come to survey the damage. In the husband's view the inspectors are more of an aggravation than the bombs.

About the Cartoonist

David Langdon was a cartoonist and illustrator whose works appeared in several British magazines and newspapers during World War II, including British humor and literary magazines *Punch* and *Lilliput*.

Chapter 4

Aftermath

Preface

World War II ended triumphantly for the Allies in Europe on May 7, 1945. However, Germany's formal surrender that day did not close the book on the actions of that nation's leaders. Between October 1945 and August 1946 unprecedented trials were held that helped create a modern understanding of human rights and war crimes. While not without their critics, who assert that the cases were flawed legally, the Nuremberg Trials proved that the men who were behind one of history's great atrocities could not escape justice.

Few trials, if any, can compare to the scope of Nuremberg. Named for the German city where they were held, the trials determined the fate of twenty-two men and six organizations. Among the defendants were Rudolf Hess, the commandant of the Auschwitz concentration camp, and Hermann Göring, one of Adolf Hitler's top aides. Hitler himself was not put on trial—he had committed suicide on April 30, 1945. The four prosecuting nations were the United States, Great Britain, France, and Russia. They formed cases against the defendants on four counts: conspiracy to wage aggressive war, waging aggressive war, war crimes, and crimes against humanity.

Proving these charges was a complicated task for the four countries. Among the stumbling blocks was the fact that European law did not cover the notion of conspiracy. In addition, Hitler's decision to wage an aggressive war did not necessarily indicate that Germany had violated prewar international agreements. Moreover, crimes against humanity had not been defined to include a government's acts against people other than its own citizens. The prosecutors overcame these difficulties, with only three of the defendants being acquitted. Eight of the convicted men received prison sentences, while the others were sentenced to death. The death sentences were carried out on October 15, 1946; however, Göring committed suicide a few hours before his scheduled execution.

The Nuremberg Trials have had a profound effect on human rights and war crimes. For example, the trials led to the establishment of the seven Nuremberg principles. The fifth of these principles states: "Any person charged with a crime under international law has the right to a fair trial on the facts and law." In the sixty years since World War II ended, several major war crime trials have been held, such as the trial of Slobodan Milosevic, the "butcher of Belgrade," who has been accused of overseeing massacres in Bosnia and Croatia. Another important principle is the fourth, which eliminates the excuse that a soldier or civilian citizen was only following orders when committing an immoral act, "provided a moral choice was in fact possible to him."

While undoubtedly influential, the Nuremberg Trials have not met with universal approval. The criticisms center largely around the beliefs that the prosecutors relied on too broad an interpretation of international laws and that the conspiracy charges were based on murky evidence. In an otherwise mostly positive analysis of the trials, history professor Michael Biddiss writes, "The Allies could have got most of what they wanted, and could have done so in a morally less dubious way, by limiting their prosecution solely to 'war crimes' and 'crimes against humanity.'"

The Nuremberg Trials are one example of the impact of the World War II, both immediately after the conclusion of the war and in the decades since. In this chapter the cartoonists examine the political and economic aftermath of World War II.

Examining Cartoon 1:
"A Just and Workable Peace"

About the Cartoon

The use of the atomic bomb on the Japanese cities of Hiroshima and Nagasaki in August 1945 was arguably the most controversial decision of the twentieth century. The bombings caused the deaths of tens of thousands of Japanese civilians and ushered in the nuclear age. In this cartoon Paul Carmack offers an image of an atomic bomb looming over a peace meeting. The bomb, which has human features, stands near some men gathered around a conference table. It warns the men that unless a just and workable peace is implemented, a dark fate is the likely result. Carmack's words proved prescient. Although World War II came to an end, the threat of nuclear warfare remained. Former Allies the United States and the Soviet Union entered into a decades-long Cold War in which both sides built up huge nuclear arsenals, creating the potential for an all-out nuclear war of global proportions. Arms control treaties between the two superpowers ended the possibility that such a war could occur between the United States and the Soviets, but nuclear weapons continue to proliferate throughout the world.

About the Cartoonist

Paul Carmack was a cartoonist for the *Christian Science Monitor*.

Examining Cartoon 2:
"We Accuse!"

About the Cartoon

The Holocaust was an attempt by Germany during World War II to kill all Jews who lived under German rule. During the first three years, the Nazis relied on troops known as the Einsatzgruppen to shoot Jews. The Nazis changed tactics in 1942 and built concentration camps. Millions of Jews were forced out of their homes and sent to these camps, where the strongest were put to work and the weakest were executed in gas chambers. Six million Jews died in these camps from poisonous gas, starvation, or disease. In addition, the Nazis killed 6 million non-Jews whom they considered undesirable, including homosexuals and Gypsies. When the scope of the Holocaust was revealed toward the end of the war, debate arose over whether the Allies should have taken action sooner to either destroy the camps or help Jews escape from Nazi-controlled Europe. The horrors of the camps also led people to exhort that genocides on such a horrifying level should never occur again, but incidents in Sudan, Cambodia, and Rwanda since World War II have shown that the world is still guilty of allowing deaths to occur on massive scales.

The first camp to be liberated by the Allies was Auschwitz, in January 1945. The liberation of the Bergen-Belsen and Buchenwald camps followed in April, with all the surviving inmates freed by the end of the war in Europe. In this cartoon an unknown Soviet artist draws a harrowing picture of starving inmates staring at their Nazi captors, silently accusing them of committing horrific crimes. The words written on the chests of four of the survivors are Russian for the concentration camps Majdanek, Treblinka, Auschwitz, and Buchenwald. These gaunt men, women, and children are drawn in sharp contrast to the corpulent Nazi officers.

About the Cartoonist

This cartoon was drawn for the Soviet satirical newspaper *Krokodil*.

My obvenyaem. *Krokodil*, Moscow, no. 20, 1945.

Examining Cartoon 3:
"The Big Three"

THE BIG THREE

About the Cartoon

Although Germany did not surrender to the Allies until May 7, 1945, the war in Europe was largely over by February of that year. Between February 4 and 11, the "Big Three"—American president Franklin D. Roosevelt, British prime minister Winston Churchill, and Soviet leader Joseph Stalin—met at Yalta to discuss the division of Germany into separate zones that would be controlled by Allied forces.

In this cartoon, which was published two days before the Yalta conference began, Sidney Strube suggests that the real "Big Three" are not those leaders, but instead the coal, plumbing, and bomb damage repair industries. The people who work in those sectors will be needed to rebuild Europe, which suffered massive damage from all of the battles and bombings. While the three figures representing the industries discuss how they will respond to the destruction, Roosevelt, Stalin, and Churchill peer around the door and wait for their turn at the table. In this way Strube implies that the physical reconstruction of Europe is more important than the political settlement. The features of the man at the window indicate that he might be Japanese prime minister Hideki Tojo, perhaps wondering who will rebuild Asia when the war ends.

About the Cartoonist

Sidney Strube was a cartoonist for the London *Daily Express* from 1912 to 1948. His cartoons were also syndicated worldwide.

Chronology

1932

November 8: Franklin Delano Roosevelt defeats incumbent Herbert Hoover in the presidential election.

1933

January 30: Adolf Hitler becomes Germany's chancellor.

1934

August 19: Hitler becomes führer of Germany.

1935

August 13: Congress passes the first Neutrality Act, which prohibits loans to belligerent parties but encourages noninvolvement in foreign affairs.

1936

March 7: German troops occupy the Rhineland.

October 25: Rome-Berlin Axis is signed.

November 3: Roosevelt is reelected president.

1937

May 1: Roosevelt signs the second Neutrality Act, which prohibits arms and loans to belligerent nations.

1938

March 12–13: Germany invades and announces *Anschluss* (union) with Austria.

September 30: England, France, Italy, and Germany sign the Munich Pact. The document gives Hitler the western third of Czechoslovakia (the Sudetenland) in return for a promise not to take any more of the land.

October 15: The Czech government resigns following Germany's occupation of the Sudetenland.

1939

March 15–16: Germany takes control of Czechoslovakia.

May 27: The *St. Louis*, a ship carrying almost one thousand Jewish refugees who are fleeing from the Nazis, arrives in Cuba, and all but twenty-two are refused admittance to Cuba and the United States, with the rest sent back to Europe.

August 23: Hitler and Soviet leader Joseph Stalin sign a nonaggression pact.

September 1: Germany attacks Poland, setting off World War II.

September 3: England, France, New Zealand, and Australia declare war on Germany.

September 5: Roosevelt declares America's neutrality.

November 4: Roosevelt signs a revised version of the Neutrality Act that lifts the arms embargo.

1940

May 10: Germany invades Belgium, France, Luxembourg, and the Netherlands, while Winston Churchill becomes Great Britain's prime minister.

June 11: Italy declares war on England and France.

June 13: Roosevelt signs a $1.3-billion defense bill.

June 14: Paris falls to Germany.

June 22: France surrenders to Germany.

July 10: The Battle of Britain begins as the German *Luftwaffe* drops thousands of bombs on English cities.

September 5: The America First Committee is officially launched.

September 15: The Battle of Britain ends, though blitzing of London continues into May 1941.

September 27: Japan joins the Axis.

November 5: Roosevelt is reelected president for an unprecedented third term.

December 17: Roosevelt submits a lend-lease proposal to Congress. The proposal calls for the United States to send supplies to Great Britain and any other nation facing Nazi aggression.

1941

March 11: Lend-Lease Act becomes law in the United States, and the nation begins to supply war materials to the Allies.

May 10–11: Nazi bombers damage Westminster Abbey, Big Ben, and the House of Commons.

June 22: Germany invades the Soviet Union.

July 24–26: The United States stops trading with Japan.

August 9–12: Roosevelt and Churchill meet off the coast of Newfoundland, Canada, and write the Atlantic Charter, under which the Allied nations promised to support the right of nations to determine how they wished to be governed.

September 1: Nazis order all Jews under their control to wear yellow stars.

October 17: Hideki Tojo becomes Japan's prime minister.

December 7: Japan bombs Pearl Harbor and declares war on United States and Great Britain.

December 8: United States and Britain declare war on Japan.

December 11: Germany and Italy declare war on the United States.

1942

January 20: Nazi officials meet to plan the "Final Solution," which was their effort to kill all of Europe's Jews.

January 26: American troops arrive in Great Britain.

February 19: Executive Order 9066 orders the internment of all Japanese Americans.

April: Japanese Americans living in the United States are sent to relocation centers.

April 9: American troops surrender to Japanese on the Bataan Peninsula, Philippines.

May 15: The Women's Army Corp is created.

May 16: After Corregidor falls to the Japanese, all American forces in the Philippines surrender.

June 4–6: United States cripples the Japanese fleet in the Battle of Midway.

June 24: General Dwight D. Eisenhower takes command of all American troops in Europe.

September 14: German troops lay siege to the Soviet city of Stalingrad, but are met with stiff resistance when they reach the center of the city eight days later.

November 8: United States invades North Africa.

1943

January 27: United States launches its first bombing attack on Germany.

February 2: Germans suffer major defeat at Stalingrad.

May 13: German and Italian troops surrender in North Africa.

July 25–26: Italian dictator Benito Mussolini is arrested and his Fascist government falls.

September 8: Italy surrenders.

October 13: Italy declares war on Germany.

1944

January 16: Eisenhower is named supreme commander of Allied forces in Europe.

January 27: Soviets end a nine-hundred-day siege by defeating the Germans at Leningrad.

June 6 (D-day): Allies launch the formal liberation of western Europe by landing on the beaches of Normandy, France.

June 15: United States bombs Tokyo.

August 21–29: Allied representatives meet in Washington, D.C., to discuss forming the United Nations.

August 25: Allies liberate Paris.

October 23–26: An American fleet annihilates a Japanese naval fleet in the Battle of Leyte Gulf, the largest naval battle of the war.

November 6: Roosevelt is elected to a fourth term.

December 16–27: The Battle of the Bulge, the war's last major German offensive, is fought in Ardennes.

1945

January 26: Soviet troops liberate the Auschwitz concentration camp.

February 4–11: Roosevelt, Churchill, and Joseph Stalin meet at Yalta and agree to divide Germany into separate zones that would be controlled by Allied forces.

February 13–14: Allies firebomb and destroy the German city of Dresden.

March 16: In a battle that costs four thousand American lives, American forces take the island of Iwo Jima.

April 12: Roosevelt dies in Warm Springs, Georgia, and is succeeded by Harry Truman; Allies liberate the Bergen-Belsen and Buchenwald concentration camps.

April 23: The Soviets enter Berlin.

April 28: Mussolini is captured and hung.

April 29: American troops liberate the Dachau concentration camp.

April 30: Soviets reach the Reichstag (parliament building) in Berlin; Hitler commits suicide in his bunker.

May 7: Germany surrenders to the Allies.

May 8: V-E (Victory in Europe) Day celebrates the conclusion of the European war.

July 1: American, British, and French troops occupy Berlin.

July 16: The first atomic bomb test is conducted in New Mexico.

July 17–August 2: Truman, Churchill, and Stalin meet at Potsdam to demand Japan's unconditional surrender and plan for peace in Europe.

August 6: Americans drop an atomic bomb on Hiroshima, Japan.

August 8: The Soviet Union declares war on Japan.

August 9: Americans drop an atomic bomb on Nagasaki, Japan.

August 14: Japan surrenders unconditionally.

August 15: V-J (Victory over Japan) Day celebrates Japan's surrender.

September 2: World War II officially ends when Japan signs final surrender terms on the American battleship *Missouri*.

October 24: The United Nations is created.

For Further Research

Books

Thomas B. Allen and Norman Polmar, *Code-Name Downfall: The Secret Plan to Invade Japan and Why Truman Dropped the Bomb.* New York: Simon & Schuster, 1995.

Simon Berthon, *Allies at War: The Bitter Rivalry Among Churchill, Roosevelt, and de Gaulle.* New York: Carroll & Graf, 2001.

John Morton Blum, *V Was for Victory: Politics and American Culture During World War II.* New York: Harcourt Brace Jovanovich, 1976.

Susan Briggs, *Home Front.* New York: American Heritage, 1975.

Len Cacutt, ed., *Decisive Battles: The Turning Points of World War II.* New York: Gallery, 1986.

Angus Calder, *The People's War: Britain, 1939–1945.* New York: Pantheon, 1969.

Winston Churchill, *Memoirs of the Second World War.* Boston: Houghton Mifflin, 1959.

Wayne S. Cole, *America First: The Battle Against Intervention, 1940–1941.* Madison: University of Wisconsin Press, 1953.

Robert Dallek, *Franklin D. Roosevelt and American Foreign Policy, 1932–1945.* New York: Oxford University Press, 1981.

Bernt Engelmann, *In Hitler's Germany: Daily Life in the Third Reich.* New York: Pantheon, 1986.

George Feldman, *Understanding the Holocaust*. Detroit: UXL, 1998.

Kathlyn Gay and Martin Gay, *World War II*. New York: Twenty-First Century, 1995.

Martin Gilbert, *Winston Churchill's War Leadership*. New York: Vintage, 2004.

Tom Harrisson, *Living Through the Blitz*. New York: Schocken, 1989.

Milan Hauner, *Hitler: A Chronology of His Life and Times*. New York: St. Martin's Press, 1983.

Edwin Palmer Hoyt, *The GI's War: The Story of American Soldiers in Europe in World War II*. New York: McGraw-Hill, 1988.

Akira Iriye, *The Origins of the Second World War in Asia and the Pacific*. London: Longman, 1987.

John Keegan, *The Second World War*. New York: Viking, 1989.

Warren F. Kimball, *The Most Unsordid Act: Lend-Lease, 1939–1941*. Baltimore: Johns Hopkins Press, 1969.

Walter Lord, *Day of Infamy*. New York: Bantam, 1991.

Robert James Maddox, *The United States and World War II*. Boulder, CO: Westview Press, 1992.

Jon Meacham, *Franklin and Winston: An Intimate Portrait of an Epic Friendship*. New York: Random House, 2003.

Samuel Eliot Morison, *History of United States Naval Operations in World War II, Volume Fourteen: Victory in the Pacific, 1945*. Boston: Little, Brown, 1961.

Arthur D. Morse, *While Six Million Died: A Chronicle of American Apathy*. New York: Ace, 1967.

G.E. Patrick Murray, *Victory in Western Europe: From D-Day to the Nazi Surrender*. New York: Metro, 1999.

Kenneth Paul O'Brien and Lynn Hudson, eds., *The Home-Front War: World War II and American Society*. Westport, CT: Greenwood Press, 1995.

Masatake Okumiya and Jiro Horikoshi, with Martin Caidin, *Zero!* New York: Ballantine, 1956.

Geoffrey Perrett, *Days of Sadness, Years of Triumph: The American People, 1939–1945*. New York: Coward, McCann, and Geoghegan, 1973.

William L. Shirer, *The Rise and Fall of the Third Reich*. New York: Simon & Schuster, 1959.

Louis L. Snyder, *The Encyclopedia of the Third Reich*. New York: Paragon House, 1989.

A.J.P. Taylor, *The Origins of the Second World War*. New York: Atheneum, 1961.

Katherine Whittemore, ed., *The World War Two Era: Perspectives on All Fronts from Harper's Magazine*. New York: Franklin Square Press, 1995.

Nancy Baker Wise and Christy Wise, *A Mouthful of Rivets: Women at Work in World War II*. San Francisco: Jossey-Bass, 1994.

Web Sites

Avalon Project: World War II, www.yale.edu/lawweb/avalon/wwii/wwii.htm. An extensive list of primary documents is available on this site, which is operated by the Yale University Law School. Among the items included are the Atlantic Charter, Germany and Japan's surrender documents, and documents pertaining to Pearl Harbor.

BBC History: World War II, www.bbc.co.uk/history/war/wwtwo. Presented by the British Broadcasting Corporation, this Web site provides essays and articles on the war and links to other World War II pages. Other features on the site include animated maps, audio files, and wartime posters.

World War II Links on the Internet, http://history.acusd.edu/gen/ww2_links.html. Hundreds of links relating to the war are available on this page. The links are organized by category, such as countries, the Holocaust, and personal narratives.

Index